DO NOT HARDEN YOUR HEART

LEBOGANG MERRIAM SEOKETSA

1

Publisher
Lebogang M. Seoketsa
11492 Phase 6
Morula View
Mabopane

Cell: 073 243 4002 / 079 981 7077

Email: seoketsalm@tut.ac.za

Cover design: DTP Technical Services
Layout: Lebogang M. Seoketsa

Printed and bound by: DTP 2 Print (011) 869 2419

ISBN: 978-0-620-50022-7

Acknowledgements
Every effort has been made to contact the owners of
copyright material, but this has not been possible in
some cases, we apologize for any copyright
infringement and would not hesitate to make any
appropriate arrangements in respect of this.

DEDICATION

Praise the Lord

I would like to honor and praise God, my Lord and Savior Jesus and the Holy Spirit who is my Teacher, my Helper, my guider and my Advocate for helping me to write this third book.

I would like to thank God and dedicate this book:

To my parents; my husband – Monty Seoketsa; our daughters – Dipolelo and Bria; and my brother David and his daughter Koketso.

To the members of "Your Burden is my Burden Ministries."

To my Pastor and his wife who are my Spiritual Parents of House of Praise Church: Pastor TL Toka and Mrs. YK Toka

To Pastor MS Mogoane of The Fountain of Praise and Worship Church and his wife Mrs. Mogoane

ACKNOWLDEGEMENT

Without the help of the Holy Spirit who was promised to us by our Lord Jesus Christ, nothing in life can be successful. This is the result of the contribution of many individuals who directly and indirectly share their gifts, talents and not forgetting wisdom of which our Lord said in **James 1:5** "If any of you lacks wisdom, he should ask God, who gives generously to all without finding fault, and it will be given to him."

I wish to thank my husband, Monty, and our daughters Dipolelo and Bria for their love, patience (fruit of the Spirit) and understanding for staying long hours on the computer, late nights and early mornings writing. This achievement is also yours.

Special thanks to Pastors, TL Toka and MS Mogoane and their wives again for listening when I always come to them for advises.

ABOUT THE AUTHOR

Dr. Lebogang Merriam Seoketsa is married to Mr. Monty Seoketsa and they are blessed with two daughters. She earned her Doctor of Ministry from Team Impact Christian University and M-Tech in Public Management from Tshwane University of Technology. She is currently working as departmental administrator and she worked as part-time lecturer in the department of Public Management - Tshwane University of Technology. She worked with different committees in different projects. She taught about deliverance to different groups. She is the founder of the ministry "Your Burden is my Burden" (Galatians 6:2). The ministry is taking care of the needy families. "I am holding on to the Word of God to carry the Great Commission."

The book "**DO NOT HARDEN YOUR HEART**" was written by the author understanding how important is it to respond to the Holy Spirit when He speaks to us. This book is based on the Scripture **Hebrews 3:7-8** "So as the Holy Spirit says: '**Today**, if you hear His voice, do not harden your hearts as when they provoked me, as in the days of trial in the wilderness. Where your fathers tried me by testing me, and saw my works for forty years."

This book was written to remind the Christians about the importance of the word **today** in this verse which is the key word and it point out necessity or importance. The Word of God does not say yesterday or tomorrow. It says **today.** There are lots of things to be taken care of today but the Word of God says "Today, if you hear His voice, do not harden your heart." If you do not do what the Lord is saying to you today you may end up losing important things in life.

God does not want to lose any of His children. It was not in the plan of God for any of His people to go to hell. He is calling His children in different ways but in this verse the Holy Spirit stresses it that today when people hear the Word of God, they must harden their hearts.

God is calling everybody with all kinds of problems not to concentrates on their problems but to listen to the Holy Spirit when He speaks to them. It is important to listen to the Holy Spirit and respond.

God is prepared to bless us according to His riches in glory. He wants us to have joy. Peace and whole life.

PREFACE

This book is about the importance of listening to the Holy Spirit when He speaks to us. God does not want any of His children to perish.

The heavy loads that the children of God are carrying must come to an end that is the plan of God. Jesus died on the cross for us to be healed. Sicknesses do not belong to our bodies as Holy Spirit is dwelling in us.

Marriage is ordained by God and God wants His children to be happy in this institution. Children are gifts from God and we must treat them love and teach them the right ways of God.

God wants us to be anxious for nothing. **Philippians 4:6** "Be anxious for nothing, but in everything by prayer and supplication, with thanksgiving, let your requests be made known to God."

Our Lord was persecuted but He did not give up on the one who send Him. Patience is the best remedy for every trouble. It make us good example for others who are looking at us. People can learn everything good from us through patience.

TABLE OF CONTENT

DO NOT HARDEN YOUR HEART

INTRODUCTION

When He, (Jesus Christ) left His disciples He said to them "If you love me, you will obey what I command. And I will ask my Father, and He will give you another Counselor to be with you **forever** – the Spirit of truth. The world cannot accept Him, because it neither sees Him nor knows Him. But you know Him, for He lives with you and will be in you. I will not leave you as orphans; I will come to you" (**John 14:15-18**).

Because of the Counselor who was promised to us forever, we are not supposed to suffer the problems of this world. Because of Holy Spirit who dwells in us, our bodies are not supposed to carry any diseases or hardness of this world.

God is calling us through this book to listen to the Holy Spirit when He speaks to us. Holy Spirit can speak to us in different ways while we are in different situations. Let us not look at our situations and circumstance and fail to listen to the Holy Spirit.

This book is for you and God will meet all your needs.

9

Matthew 11:28-30 "Come to me, you all who are weary and burdened, and I will give you rest. Take my yoke upon and learn from me, I am gentle and humble in heart and you will find rest for your souls. For my yoke is easy and my burden is light."

Isaiah 53:5 "But He (Jesus) was pierced for our transgressions, He was crushed for our iniquities; the punishment that brought us peace was upon Him, and by His wounds we are **healed.**"

God has ordained and blessed marriage. "The Lord God said, it is not good that man should be alone; I will make him a helper suitable for him" (**Genesis 2:18**).

Are you facing divorce? **Malachi 2:16** "I hate divorce, says the Lord of Israel." But God does not hate you.

If your partner is giving you headache, if your children are troublesome, if you are rejected, if the devil is not giving a chance, if you are the only one in the family being born again or if you are about to give up on God; this book is for you, you have all the answers and I am praying for your needs to be met. Read this book prayerfully with expectancy and the Lord will meet your needs.

1. DO NOT HARDEN YOUR HEART?

As you read this book today, do not harden your heart. "So as the Holy Spirit says: '**Today**, if you hear His voice, do not harden your hearts as when they provoked me, as in the day of trial in the wilderness. Where your fathers tried me by testing me, and saw my works for forty years." **(Hebrews 3: 7-8).** Children of Israel tested God and challenged His authority by rebelling in the wilderness and because of their rebellion; they failed to reach the rest of Canaan. God loved them and took them out of Egypt where they were slaves but they did not trust the Lord.

Today is the key word and it points out necessity or importance. The Word of God does not say yesterday or tomorrow. It says **today**. There are lots of things to be taken of today but the Word of God says "**Today**, if you hear His voice, do not harden your heart." If you do not do what the Lord is saying to you today you may end up losing important things in life.

Do not let your today to be over before you decide. Do not harden your heart because hardening the heart is not only time wasting but also dangerous as we do not know what will happen tomorrow.

Psalm 14:1 The fool says in his heart, there is no God." Let us not be like fools who are deceived by the Devil and believe what the Devil is saying to them. The Bible teaches us in **John 1:1-3** "In the beginning was the Word, and the Word was with God and the Word was God. He was with God in the Beginning. Through Him all things were made, without Him all things could have never been made that has been made. In Him was life, and the life was the light of men." The fool that says there is no God is not aware that he was created by God. Do not be like a fool and harden your heart.

Psalm 62:8 "Trust in him at all times, O people pour out your hearts to Him, for God is our refuge." God loves us and He cannot leave us no forsake us. We must trust in Him at all the times; not during certain times only. Whether things are going well or not, we must trust in Him because everything happens at its own season and those seasons are created by God Himself. There is a reason why you are in that situation and still you have to trust in him.

Psalm 37:3-4 "Trust in the Lord and do good; dwell in the land and enjoy safe pasture. Delight yourself in the Lord and he will give you the desires of your heart." By doing good is to listen to the voice of the Lord today. We must not harden our hearts and expect our Lord to give us the desires of our hearts. **Proverbs 3:5** "Trust in the Lord with all your heart and lean not on your own understanding." Our understandings sometimes make us to reason with the Holy Spirit. Reasoning with the Holy Spirit is the same as reason with God because our God is a Spirit – Holy Spirit.

1 kings 8:39 "But your hearts must be fully committed to the Lord our God, to live by His decrees and obey His commands, as at this time." We must guard our hearts not to loose any single string. Our hearts must be fully committed to our Lord because He is fully committed to us. He loved us so much that He sends His only son to save us. This is a full commitment to the people one loves.

Colossians 3:1-14 "Since, then you have been raised with Christ, set your hearts on the things of the above, where Christ is seated at the right hand of God. Set your minds on the things above not on earthly things.

For you died, and your life is now hidden with Christ in God. When Christ, who is your life, appears, then you also will appear with him in glory. Put on death, therefore, whatever belongs to your earthly nature: sexual immorality, impurity, lust, evil desires and greed, which is idolatry. Because of these, the wrath of God is coming.

You used to walk in these ways, in the life you once lived. But now you must rid yourselves of all such things as these: anger, rage, malice, slander and filthy language form your lips. Do not lie to each other, since you have taken off your old self with it practice and have put on the new self, which is being renewed in knowledge in the image of its Creator.

Here there is no Greek or Jew, circumcised or uncircumcised, barbarian, Scythian, slave or free, but Christ is all and is in all. Therefore as God's chosen people, holy and dearly loved, clothe yourselves with compassion, kindness, humility, gentleness and patience.

Bear each other and forgive whatever grievances you may have against one another. Forgive as the Lord forgave you. And over all these virtues put on love, which binds them all together in perfect unity." God loves us and He does not want to lose any of us. The Word of God teaches us that we are not of this world and we must not fix our eyes on the things of the earth. We must fix our eyes on the things of above.

People are worried that; how can we fix our eyes on the things of the above where as we are still leaving on this earth. "Since, then you have been raised with Christ, set your hearts on the things of the above, where Christ is seated at the right hand of God. Set your minds on the things above not on earthly things." (**Colossians 3:1-).**

Psalm 51:10 "Create in me a pure heart, O God, and renew a steadfast spirit within me." We must ask God to create pure hearts in us. The pure hearts created by God will help us not to harden our hearts.

Ezekiel 36:26-27 "I will give you a new heart and put on a new spirit; I will remove from you your heart of stone and give you a heart of flesh. And I will put my Spirit in you and move you to follow my decrees and be careful to keep my laws. We must depend on God to give us hearts that will not be hard. God loves us and He has good plans for us. **Jeremiah 29:11-13** "For I know the plans I have for you, plans to prosper you and not to harm you, plans to give you hope and a future. Then you will call upon me and come and pray to me, and I will listen to you."

Let us pray: Dear Lord Jesus Christ, be with me and help me to understand every single word that you say through this book. Give me a new heart and put on the new Spirit in me. Remove from me the heart of stone and give me the heart of flesh so that I do not harden my heart. I would like to respond to every word you are saying to me so that I may leave a changed life. I ask all these in the name of our Lord and Savior Jesus Christ - Amen.

2. ARE YOU TIRED AND HEAVY LOADED?

The tiredness in our bodies can be the results of different things. Worrying about the future, worrying about our children, our marriages, sicknesses in our bodies, our families, etc. These problems carry on until we do not have strength anymore. In most cases we are worrying about things we need not to worry about. We do not keep our eyes on the Lord and we always try to solve the problems on our own.

The Bible tells us that "Therefore I say to you, do not worry about your life, what you will eat or what you will drink or about your body, what you will put on. Is not life more important than food and the body more important than clothing? Look at the birds of the air; for they neither sow nor reap no gather into barns; yet your heavenly Father feeds them. Are you not of more value that they? Which of you by worrying can add one cubit to his stature? So why do you worry about clothing? Consider the lilies of the field, how they grow: they neither toil nor spin; and yet I say to you that even Solomon in all his glory was not arrayed like one of these" **(Matthew 6:25-29)**. Worries do not improve our lives. They cause us depression and other sicknesses. When we worry too much we become tired. We become weary and heavy loaded.

Matthew 11:28-30 "Come to me you all who are weary and burdened, and I will give you rest. Take my yoke upon and learn from me, I am gentle and humble in heart and you will find rest for your souls for my yoke is easy and my burden is light."

Are you tired? The Lord says "**come to me**" today. Do not harden your heart. If you hear what the Lord is saying. The Lord knows you and He is aware that you are tired. What you can only do is to humble yourself, rise up your hands, cry to Him and tell Him that you cannot handle it any longer. The Lord is ready at all the times to help us. The Lord is not referring us to someone else but He is saying "come to me" not to anybody else but to Him.

Some of the heavy loads we are carrying cannot be off loaded by anything else except Jesus Christ. "He gives strength to the weary and increases the power to the weak. Even youths grow tired and weary, and young men stumble and fall; but those who hope in the Lord will renew their strength. They will soar on wings like eagles; they will run and not grow weary, they will walk and not be faint" (**Isaiah 40:29-31**).

Come to me you **all who are weary and burdened.** God is aware of the burden on us. He is calling you because He is aware that you are weary and burdened. He is not calling those who are happy. He knows that they do not seek Him but you, because you need Him, He is calling you by purpose. He is aware that you are hopeless and you cannot help yourself.

God is promising to give us rest. He says "**I will give you rest take my yoke upon**". No rest is rest if it is not from God. In most of the times we become tired because we do not have enough time with God. We concentrate on serving or doing a lot of work and not giving us time to worship God. Those who typically do not have problems like suffering depression and worry are those who serve, love and worship the Lord. They study the Word of God, cast their burdens off to God and when they do the work, they are the happiest people working for the Lord.

We are looking for the things of this world and forgetting to focus on the owner of the world. We become tired because we do not seek God first. The Bible teaches us to seek first the kingdom of God and His righteousness and all these things shall be added. **Matthew**

6:33 "But seek first His Kingdom and His righteousness, and all these things will be given to you as well." All these things are all you need. God knows our needs and He gives the desires of our hearts. He knows that you are tired and you need to rest.

The good example is at the home of Martha and Mary: **Luke 10:38-42** "As Jesus and his disciples were on their way, He came to a village where a woman named Martha opened her home to Him. She has a sister called Mary, who sat at the Lord's feet listening to what He said. But Martha was distracted by all the preparation that had to be made. She came to Him and asked, 'Lord, don't you care that my sister has left me to do the work by myself? Tell her to help me!' "Martha, Martha" the Lord answered, "you are worried and upset about many things, but only one thing is needed. **Mary has chosen what is better** and it will not be taken away from her."

Martha was worried about many things which were not important at that time. She was busy with the preparation and that was not the time for preparations. Mary has chosen what is better and it will not be taken from her. She chose to be with the Lord. The Lord knows our needs. God wants us to be with Him. In most of the times we concentrate on the work and forget to give ourselves time with God. If we give ourselves time with God, we will have enough rest but if choose to concentrate on the work and keep on worrying about many things, we will be weary and burdened.

The Lord wants us to learn from Him. In Mathew the Lord is asking us to **learn from Him.** We must allow Holy Spirit to speak to our heart to encourage us and help us to solve our problems. Our Lord wants us to come to Him. He knows that we are tired and burdened by heavy loads that are not necessary.

Our Lord carries our burdens on daily basis. **Psalms 68:19** "Praise be to the Lord, God our Savior, who daily bears and burdens." Holy Spirit is ready to lead us through every day of our lives so that we can have rest and peace.

God cannot sustain us until we cast our entire burden on Him. **Psalms 55:22** "Cast your burden on the Lord, and He shall sustain you; He shall never permit the righteous to be moved." When we keep our burdens, it means we are trying to sustain ourselves. We cannot sustain ourselves we will eventually fall flat on our faces and get tired and weary. We must not try to handle the burdens ourselves. We must cast them all to the Lord.

We must cast all our care upon Him. **1 Peter 5:7** "Cast all your care upon Him, for He cares for you." God is commanding us not to worry. He is not requesting us. God wants us to be anxious for nothing. **Philippians 4:6** "Be anxious for nothing, but in everything by prayer and supplication, with thanksgiving, let your requests be made known to God."

Do not harden your heart. Take the first step. Come to Jesus so He can set you free from any and all burdens that you are carrying. Call His Name for help; He is always ready to help you. You must be ready for His divine intervention.

Let us pray: Dear Lord Jesus Christ, thank you for carrying the burden which was heavy for me. Help me to be anxious for nothing, but in everything by prayer and supplication, with thanksgiving, help me to make my requests be known to you my God. Help me not to depend on myself as your Word teaches us to trust in you with all our hearts. Help me not to lean on my understanding. I ask you to be with me in Jesus Name, Amen.

3. ARE YOU SICKNESS?

I am worried and really worried about people who are sick whereas we have JESUS CHRIST as our Healer. If we believe in Jesus Christ and believe that He died for us on the Cross, then healing is for us. Our healing and eternal life was provided on the Cross. The body of Jesus Christ was broken for every natural thing we need. There is no need for us to get sick.

Jesus Christ is our Healer, our Jehovah Rapha, and the Lord who heals. If we call on the Name of our Lord Jesus Christ, we know that we get everything we need; healing, forgiveness, peace, divine protection and we are also saved.

Most of people think that the healing of sickness provided by Jesus Christ was for the people of those olden days. Even today, Jesus Christ heals. There can be things in our lives that stop the healing power of God – Lord Jesus Christ. God is not withholding healing from us. The same God who gives unconditional forgiveness of sins is the same God who heals us unconditionally from every disease and sickness.

Isaiah 53:5 "But He (Jesus) was pierced for our transgressions, He was crushed for our iniquities; the punishment that brought us peace was upon Him, and by His wounds we are **healed."**

If you are seeking any kind of healing from the Lord, this book is for you. Healing is rightfully yours and you must claim it in the name of Jesus Christ. God promised us healing and we must believe that He keeps His promises.

The Devil has no legal right to make you sick because the price has already been paid. You are a free person. Refuse to be sick and claim your healing in the name of Jesus. God did not intend for us to be sick or suffer in any way. God hates sicknesses and diseases because they came as a result of sin. The sin that was committed for the first time in the Garden of Eden.

Man was commanded not to eat the tree of the knowledge of good and evil. **Genesis 2:17** "but you must not eat from the tree of the knowledge of good and evil, for when you eat of it you will surely die." Death came through Adam and life through Jesus. Jesus Christ came into the world to destroy these works of the devil and restore mankind to fellowship in harmony with God the Creator. Through the work of the cross, every believer can attain physical healing.

Jesus wants us to be well. He wants the sick to be healed. During His ministry on earth He healed everybody who believed in Him. He instructed us to do the same. This shows that Jesus Christ had compassion on people and He does not want to see people being sick. It pleases God to see His people being free from the oppression of the devil.

Christ has already paid the price for your healing. He does not want to see you suffer again. It pains Jesus Christ to see you lining in the bed, full of pain. Jesus Christ wants to set you free so that you can serve Him well with joyful heart. The Devil is full of jealous. He wants to destroy you so that you cannot serve your God.

God gives us the desires of our hearts. **Psalms 37:4** "Delight yourself in the Lord and He will give you the desires of your heart." You must have the desire to be healed. God can only heal you if you desire to be healed. Sometimes men and women of God pray for the sick people and they do not get healed because it is not their desire to be healed. Some people do not want to be healed because they want attention from people.

They enjoy being sick because they get all attention from people.

Some people who are earning grants for their sickness, they also do not want to get healed because they do not want to forfeit their grants. Now you will find that the family members are the one who want them to be healed but they (the sick people) do not want to be healed. God will never heal you if it is not your desire to be healed. Sicknesses belong to the Devil and we must hate them because they stop us from serving our Lord.

You are the King's child. The blood of Jesus Christ was shed on the cross for you and me to get healed. The King's child has the right to ask anything from the King. **Matthew 7:7-8** "Ask and it will be given to you; seek and you will find; knock and the door will be opened for you. For everyone who asks receives, he who seeks finds; and to him who knocks, the door will be opened."

You are to ask specific things but to ask anything. Jesus Christ our Healer told us in the book of **John 14:13** "And I will do whatever you ask in my name so that the Son may bring glory to the Father." God cannot heal you if you do not ask. God cannot heal you if you ask but you do not have faith. The

Devil will not leave you if you do not confess the Word of God.

The Devil knows that by His stripes we are healed but if you do not confess those words, he (Devil) will whisper and lie to you that you will not get healed and you are going to die. Face the Devil fearlessly by telling him that Greater is He that is in you than the one that is in the world. Tell the Devil that no weapon formed against you shall proper. Tell the Devil that Jesus Christ has given the authority to trample on the snakes and the scorpions; the poison will do you no harm. No sickness will let you lie on bed denying you to serve your Father.

In the book of **2 Kings 7:3-4**; we read about four men who were stricken by leprosy. "Now there were four men with leprosy at the entrance of the city gate. They said to each other, 'why stay here until we die? If we say, we'll go into the city – the famine is there, and we will die. And if we stay here, we will die. So let's go over to the camp of the Arameans and surrender. If they spare us, we live; if they kill us, then we die."

These men were sick and the devil confirmed to them that they are going to die. They did not know that God has already healed them and God is ready to use them. When you are lying on your bed waiting for your death which was confirmed by the devil, you are wasting the time of God. God has already healed you and He is waiting for you to stand up and go to do His work.

The four leprosy men deliver the people of Israel from the severe famine of during that time. By standing where they were intending to surrender to Arameans, God used them and the people of Israel were delivered from poverty. God has the work for you like the leprosy men. There are people out there who must be helped by you and you are the only one that God wants to send. If you do not listen to what the Holy Spirit is saying to you by hardening your heart, you will not be healed. Do not harden you heart, God has healed you, stand up and serve Him.

I believe God for your healing and I do not care how many times you were told that you are going to die because of that sickness. God is your creator. I am taking you back to Him to repair you. The creators of Nissan Qashqai are the only ones who can repair it better than anyone else. The creators of BMW X5 are the only ones who can repair it better than anyone else. Now God is the only one who can repair you better because He is your Creator.

James 5:15 "The prayer of faith shall save the sick, and the Lord shall raise him up..." God's Word should never be doubted. God cannot lie. He is not a person that He should lie. **Numbers 23:19** "God is not a man, that He should lie, nor a son of man that he should change His mind." He heals all our diseases and we should praise Him. **Psalms 103:2-3** "Praise the Lord, O my soul, and forget not all His benefits – who forgives all your sins and heals all your diseases." The Bible tells that He heals all our diseases. This means that no matter what disease you may be suffering from, God heals.

My husband got sick in October 2009. He was admitted in one of clinic in our area and I had doubts that I could have taken him to another clinic. When the doctor admitted him, he was in terrible condition but the doctor did not want to let me know how terrible the condition was. He suffered from appendix which busted before he could be operated. I, together with other women of God prayed and asked for his healing because in His word He says "ask and it shall be given to you" (Matthew 7:7). **James 5:15** "The prayer of faith shall save the sick, and the Lord shall raise him up..."

In the middle of the night of the same day he was admitted, when I was praying, claiming his healing, I heard the Lord speaking to me. He said "Akasia clinic or Odi hospital, I am the one who heals." God knows what is in our hearts and what we think. I doubted the clinic he was admitted at but I did not tell anybody. God gives us the desires of our hearts. My husband was admitted for eleven days and he stayed at home for the whole month before he could go to work. I thank God because he is healed.

God wants us to enjoy good health and that all may go well with us even as our soul is getting along well. **3 John 2** "Beloved, I wish above all things that thou mayest proper and be in health, even as thy soul prospeth." It is the will of our Lord that we have excellent health.

God had not changed. He is still the same God of today and yesterday. If He healed people previous years and yesterday, He can still heal you today. He declared in **Exodus 15:26** "....for I am the Lord who heals you." The Bible tells us that the Lord is the one who heals us not anyone else.

God promised us healing and that healing is still valid. God promised us that He is not a changing God. "I the Lord do not change" (**Malachi 3:6**).

Pray with me this prayer: Dear Lord Jesus, I believe that you are my Creator, my Healer and my Provider. I come before you right now in the Name of Jesus Christ and as your word say ask it shall be given to you, I am asking that you heal me right now in Jesus Name. I believe that no weapon formed against me shall prosper and you are greater than the Devil who is in the world. I know that sicknesses are not from you and I surrender myself before you so that you take care of me.

Accept my prayer and heal me in Jesus Name. Cleanse me and help me to serve. Help me to glorify you at all the times with everything I do. I thank you for the divine healing and I refuse to accept the devil's dirty works anymore in Jesus Name - Amen.

4. IS YOUR MARRIAGE GOING DOWN THE DRAIN?

No marriage is without turbulence. In all marriages there are misunderstandings over small issues. If tiffs are more than happy times, then it is time to Break Barriers and build the bridges. Do not neglect your marriage because it will be ruined.

Marriage is the institution created by God the Creator of everything. It must be respected as the owner of marriage is respectful. God is not happy to see the marriages of His children going down the drain and ending up in divorce. The marriage which is going down the drain is at better stage than the stage of divorce. Facing divorce will be discussed in the next chapter.

It is my prayer as you read this book that if you are facing this stage; you come to your senses and see how important your marriage is. "Dear Lord, I am praying for the person who is reading this book and facing this stage to realize how important marriage is. Help him/her to play an important role in saving his/her marriage because at this stage many people are affected and not only people who are facing this stage. Heal everybody who is affected and restore this marriage in Jesus name."

God has ordained and blessed marriage. "The Lord God said, it is not good that man should be alone; I will make him a helper suitable for him" (**Genesis 2:18**). From the beginning God said "it is not good for a man to be alone." And He made him a suitable helper. The wife or the husband you are staying with is suitably made for you. It is not a mistake. God will never lie. He is not a man that He should lie or a son that He should change His mind.

Sometimes marriages are going down the drains because husbands and wives missed it somewhere. In the beginning there was love, understanding, respect, peace, harmony, lovemaking and submission. If one of the things I mentioned here is missing, wakeup; your marriage is going down the drain. Do not harden your heart because the Holy Spirit is speaking to you to save your marriage.

Adulate/adore: In marriage there must be love there must be adulation. Marriage without love is a disaster. It is a failure. Sometimes there is this feeling that women love more than men. That is why the word of God teaches us in **Ephesians 5:25, 28** "Husbands, love your wives, even as Christ also loved the church and gave Himself for it. Husbands ought to love their wives as their own bodies. He who loves his wife loves himself." Husbands must not just love their wives; they must also give themselves to them.

In my first book "Enjoying the fruit of the Spirit" I like the part where I talk about love. "Love is patient, love is kind. It does not envy, it does not boast, it is not proud. It is not rude, it is not self-seeking, it is not easily angered, and it keeps no record of wrongs. Love does not delight in evil but rejoices with the truth. It always protects, always trusts, always hopes and always perseveres. Love never fails. And now these three remain: faith, hope and love. But the greatest of these is love" (**1 Corinthians 13:4-8, 13**).

Colossians 3:19 "Husbands, love your wives and do not be harsh with them." Do not be bitter against them. Husbands must praise, honor and please their wives. Always congratulate your wife, praise her on all good things she is doing for you and your children. Show her how important she is to you and your children. "But a married man is concerned about the affairs of this world – how he can please his wife" (**1 Corinthians 7:33**).

Wives are important to their husbands just as husbands to their wives. The Bible tells us that "He who finds a wife finds what is good and receives favor from the Lord" (**Proverbs 18:22**). You as a wife to your husband; you are important and you are his crown. "A wife of noble character is her husband's crown" (**Proverbs 12:4**). Even if your husband cannot see that; you must know it, that because of your noble character you are his crown.

Wives are also to love and please their husbands. They must understand that the head of the woman is man – her husband. "For a man did not come from a woman, but a woman from man; neither was man created for a woman but a woman for a man" (**1 Corinthians 11:8-9).** "A kindhearted woman gain respect" (**Proverbs 11:16).**

It is important that we always make our love known towards those who mean the most to us. We must not come into the stage where we get into a routine in life and neglect those who are most near and dear to us. We must not assume that they know how we feel about them. To say "I love you" or "I really care about", it is something that one has to sweat for. We must be used to these words and express our feeling to our loved ones. Let this be a habit! A habit of saying loving and sweet words will build good relationships between couples and others who relate to you.

The Word of God teaches to guard our tongues. "Let no corrupt communication proceed out of your mouth, but that which is good to the use of edifying, that it may minister grace unto the hearers. And grieve not the Holy Spirit of God, whereby ye are sealed unto the day of temptation. Let all bitterness, and wrath, and anger and clamor and evil speaking, be put way from you, with all malice: And be ye kind one to another, tenderhearted, forgiving one another, even as God for Christ's sake hath forgiven you." (**Ephesians 4:29-32**). Sometimes by corrupt communication we grieve the Holy Spirit. But if we say loving words, the Holy Spirit will not be grieved.

Admiration and Obedience (respect and submission: Wives must be respectful and submissive to their husband. This is scriptural. **Colossians 3:18** "Wives submit to your husbands as is fitting in the Lord." **Ephesians 5:22-23** "Wives, submit to your husbands as to the Lord. For the husband is the head of the wife as Christ is the head of the church, his body of which He is the Savior." Sometimes people take submission as something makes you very low. People think that you can only be submissive to your husband if he is only of high class or occupying high positions with high levels of qualifications.

God is not looking at world things. We; as children of God, we do not look at the things of this world. God gave you that partner without looking at the things of this world. As a wife, regardless of the positions and status of your husband, submit yourself to him. **1 Peter 3:1-6** "Wives in the same way be submissive to your husband.....in a meek and quite spirit in the sight of the Lord." Wives should not be loud and stubborn. They should be guidance in their home and children.

Respect sometime is taken for granted. Partners do not respect each other the way they should. We should respect our partners the way we respect others. The golden rule is respect others to be respected. I say respect your partner so that you can be respectful not forgetting others. In strengthening and repairing our marriages, we must show respect to each other. There is no person who does not want to be respected. Respect is a powerful tool in healthy and harmonious relationship. "A kindhearted woman gain respect" **(Proverbs 11:16).** "Show proper respect to everyone" (**1 Peter 2:17**)

Tranquility and Accord - (Peace and Harmony): These two are important in marriages. In marriage strives and quarrels must be avoided. You are chosen people of God. God saw fit that you should be husband and wife. "Therefore as chosen people of God, holy and dearly loved, clothe yourselves with compassion, kindness, humility, gentleness and patience. Bear with each other and forgive whatever grievances you may have against one another" (**Colossians 3:13**).

Getting to know each other in marriage (Lovemaking in Marriage): Sex in **MARRIAGE** is pure, holy and ordained by God. Lovemaking out of marriage is a sin. Here we are building marriage which is going down the drain not a relationship out of marriage. We are building marriage which was once blessed by God and now the Devil being busy destroys it. In marriage; husband and wife are joined together as one. "But at the beginning of creation God made them male and female. For this reason a man will leave his father and mother and be united to his wife, and the two will become one flesh. So they are no longer two but one. Therefore what God has joined together, let man not separate" (**Mark 10:6-9**). When the two are joined together and ordained by God, they are free to enjoy what God has allowed them to do.

Husband is free to sleep on the breast of his wife. **Proverbs 5:19** "A loving doe, a graceful deer – may her breast satisfy you always, may you ever be captivated by her love." Husband and wives must not take lovemaking as punishment or reward for something. If a wife has done something wrong then the husband will want to punish her in the bed. Again if husband has to enjoy his marital right then he has to do something so that he can be rewarded by sex. **1 Corinthians 7:3-4** "The husband should fulfill his marital duty to his wife and likewise the wife to the husband. The wife's body does not belong to her alone but also to her husband. In the same, the husband's body does not belong to his alone but also to his wife." Husbands and wives must live to please God. Husbands should treat their wives with honor and love.

If your marriage is going down the drain because of all things mentioned above, do not harden your heart. It is time for you to check where it went wrong. It is not too late. Go back to God and ask for forgiveness. Ask God for the restoration of everything. The love you used to love your husband/wife is no more. Ask God for the restoration of that first love again. The respect you use to give your spouse is no more; ask God to help you to respect your spouse again. You used to be submissive to your husband but today you take your husband as a mere toy or boy. God will never fail you. Turn to Him and tell Him that you want to be submissive to your husband. You cannot be submissive to Lord Jesus Christ whereas you are not submissive to your husband as the Word of God tells us. **Ephesians 5:22-23** "Wives, submit to your husbands as to the Lord. For the husband is the head of the wife as Christ is the head of the church, his body of which He is the Savior."

Your family used to be in peace and harmony. Today there is no peace in the house. Every one in the house is taking his/her direction. No one can restore that. Only God can. Ask God to restore that peace, that harmony that love, that respect and those smiles that used to be on your faces. Husbands/wives; enjoy what God legally gave you. Husbands; enjoy the water of your own cistern and enjoy it. Your wife was given to you By God. Also wife, you husband has been given to you by God. Do not let troubles and trials of this world separate you. Be together in everything you do. You are joined by God and no man should separate you.

Avoiding booming/crashing on the communication highway

Healthy marriages require **time, attention, energy and vigilance/care**. It needs effort to have a super marriage.

Do not run marriage like a business. Marriage is of God and He is the one who can service it better than anyone else.

1. Never say there is **nothing wrong** when there is something to wrong.
   - If you see your spouse upset, do not agree with him/her when he/she says there is nothing wrong.
   - Wives in particular like to say there is nothing wrong even if things are not right.
2. Never say "**ok its fine**" whilst your spouse can detect from your tone that it is not fine.
   - Your tone and non-verbal communication make it clear to your spouse that it is not fine.
3. Partners must be **committed in their marriage**. Be free when you are doing anything on the computer. Being anxious when your spouse comes next to you when working on the computer or

talking on the phone may cause conflict in marriage. Some say that there is nothing wrong but being involved with someone online takes marriage's commitment.

4. It is not good to answer each others' cell phone but for a partner to answer his/her cell in the closet is unhealthy. To be on a safer side do not answer your partner's cell phone and again do not jump into conclusion. **Trust your partner**.

There are temptations of lust/covet in marriage – avoid them

1. **Make your marriage priority number one- (Let it be your main concern):** Let your spouse come first. Follow the order of God:
   - God
   - Spouse - Family
   - Others – **Ministry** if you are God's servant, relatives, friends or job.
     - Do not find yourself in a situation where your friends and relatives come first or are dominating in your marriage.
     - Be committed to each other. Let your time, energy and effort be in your marriage.

2. **Cherish, develop, cultivate and look after the emotional intimacy or relationship in your marriage:**
   - Talk to each everyday about everything including your feelings.
   - Share everything, your joy, your fears, your frustrations, your disappointments and your challenges.
   - Let your spouse know and realize how much value you give to him/her. This level of talking or having time for each other connects you into a deeper level.
3. **Appreciate/value each other at all the times**:
   - The word of God teaches us to be thankful at all the times. **1 Thessalonians 5:18 "Give thanks in all circumstances...."**
   - Give thanks and compliments to each other. To say thank you is not expensive.
   - Appreciate every little thing your spouse is doing for you and your family. This may include:
     - ➢ Cooking meals for the family
     - ➢ Taking kids to bed
     - ➢ Doing laundry
     - ➢ Giving a glass of water or any drink

- ➤ Collecting you from work to home
- ➤ Taking you to church or to anywhere
- ➤ Everything that your spouse is doing must be appreciated even if he/she is not doing for you.
- ➤ Sometimes your spouse might be doing something for your family, friends or any one you know.
- Tell your spouse how much you love, admire and respect him/her. Tell him/her as many times as you can. Do not worry how many times you tell him/her per day. He/she is your partner and he/she expect those words from you. If you do not give your spouse those words, he/ he will get them outside and this is the beginning of all bad things.
- You cannot change your partner but you can change yourself.
- Love him/her because he/she is the person you chose to spend life with. Accept him/ her.
- The devil looks for the loop holes and once he gets them, he uses them.

4. Are your priorities the same?
Togetherness in marriages glue

spouses but a **gap** give the third person a chance:

When two people in marriage have separate priorities, it shows lack of time for each other, children ignored and different agendas.

- Give your marriage time of being together, doing things together, going out, relaxing, going for a picnic, going to a restaurant, and also hanging our together.
- If you do not do these things together, you are opening a **loop hole** and the third person will enter.
- Every minute of your time must not be rushed or tightly scheduled. If time is scheduled for yourselves, spend it wisely and enjoy every second.
- Staying connected to God and to each other is the most important ingredient in marriage

5. **Keep your sex life active: (Let your feelings respond to each other at all the times)**
   - There are things that make partners not to enjoy their sex life any more than they used to.
     - Sicknesses, stress, tiredness, fatigue, unresolved issues and children who are troublesome.

> Be patient with each other when times like these come.
> Be there for each other and show love to your spouse.

When there is no love, patience or tolerance to one partner who is sick, your marriage is in danger.

6. Discuss/share and resolve issues as they come:
- Do not hide issues and problems.
- Be open with each other so that it can be easy for you to solve the problems.
- Do not suspend the issues.
- Do not sleep or spend the night with unresolved issues.

7. Affirmation/Acknowledgement:
- Sometimes people see negative things more than positive things. Always point out positive things your spouse is doing or have done.
- It is important to see good things your spouse is doing and always tell you spouse how best he/she is.
- To tell your spouse that you are a good parent, daddy or sweet somebody is important.

- Let your partner know that everything he/she is doing for your family is appreciated.

8. Approval/Support:
- Let your partner know that you are committed to him/her.
- Approve to him/ her that you speak good of him/her all the times
- If there are some of the things you are not approving, look for those you approve and make them known to others.
- Do not keep quite because keeping quite is the way to the death of your marriage.

9. Affection/Love/Fondness/Care – this is a romantic one and it arouses the feelings:
- Give a lot of touch because this reduces tension, tiredness and restlessness.
- Give each other more of touching even outside bedroom.
  - ➤ Give hugs
  - ➤ Kiss at all the times
  - ➤ Hold each others hands when you are walking together
  - ➤ Reduce tension from your partner by hugging him/her and

tell him/ her "I love you." If there is nothing to say just say "I love you". Get used to this.

➢ Touch each other when watching TV
➢ This touching will cultivate the sexual parts.

10.   Attention/Concentration/Consideration

- Eye contact is important.
- It is important to look in each other's' eyes when talking to each other.
- Do not talk to your spouse whilst in another room. Eye contact is important.
- Look at your spouse with eyes that show that you see something and your ears must hear everything your partner is saying.

Follow what has been said above and try to change your marriage. Marriage is the institution of God our Creator and He will help you if you ask Him.

Marital Communication: Communication in marriage is a sensitive tool that can course damage if couples are not aware. There is a way of communicating with your spouse, children, roommate and anybody else. Couples must understand each other and know how to communicate with each other. Silence or withdrawing from communication is not the way to solve problems. Instead it is the worst and painful way of treating your partner which can lead to divorce. If communications dries up, spouses become thirsty and they slowly die as their most needs are not met.

Communication cannot work on itself. It needs someone to work on it. Understand your spouse and know how to communicate with her/him. Differentiate from talking to you spouse, to your children and to other people. Make communication sweet and entertaining to your spouse. Never belittle your spouse at all the times. Not in front of his/her friends, children or anybody of whatever kind. Never let any name calling come out of your mouth under any circumstances. "Don't use foul or abusive language. Let everything you say be good and helpful, so that your words will be an encouragement to those who hear them."

Get to know your spouse and cultivate an intimacy that is deeper than sex. Get to know his/her feelings, thoughts, desires and dreams as though they were your own. Share and work on them together. On sharing your dreams, listen to each other and evaluate which one to be handled first. Take one dream at the time.

Never raise your voice. It is a sign of disrespect. This is a problem which most women struggle from. When there is a problem in the house you will hear by high voices raised to someone in that house. Nowadays our children, who attend model c schools, cannot handle it when we talk to them. I used to hear my friend complaining that every time she talks to her daughter when she is mistaken, her daughter would say, "Do not shout at me, your voice is too high for my ears." Her mother would try to explain to her that, "that is the way she talked, her voice is high and there is nothing she can do about it."

"A gentle answer turns away wrath, but a harsh word stirs up anger" (**Proverbs 15:1**). I also used to have this kind of a problem. When talking to my husband sometimes when responding to what he was saying to him, my voice would be high unaware and when he says to me that my voice is high, I would say "No my voice is not high, that is the way I am." But I prayed God to help me in this problem and in most cases before I can answer or respond to what he is saying even if provoking, I would keep quite first or take my time then respond later. I learned how to listen before I can talk. The Bible teaches us that "Everyone should be quick to listen, slow to speak and slow to become angry, for man's anger does not bring about the righteous life that God desires" (**James 1:19-20**). This is true, answering in anger normally causes people to raise voices. I learned to be slow to become angry. It was not a simple thing but God helped me a lot in this case. When I am angry I keep quiet and during that time, it is the time where I speak with my God, asking for forgiveness even if I am not the one who caused the problem.

People have never realized how good is it to ask for forgiveness even if you are not mistaken. You become free and the burden on your shoulder will be off loaded.

Avoid talking about other people in a negative way to your spouse. Always say good things about people. If there is nothing good to say about others; just do not say anything.

If you say something bad about others to your spouse, she/he will think that when you are with others, you say something bad about him/her or your relatives. Talk about love, encouragements, building relationships, motivating people, praying for people, etc.

If your partner is negative on those things, you are in trouble. Therapy is needed. We must not forget that our marriages are built on the foundation of God. We must not forget that there is no good relationship.

Relationships differ just as people differ. There cannot always be good times in relationship. There is going to be a time where couples experience bad times. During these bad times things will change. Just as good time did not last long, also bad time will pass and time for something will come. Seasons come and pass. Seasons stay for the time created by God even times in relationships will come and pass.

"There is a time for everything and a season for every activity under heaven. A time to be born and a time to die, a time to plant and a time to uproot, a time to kill and a time to heal, a time to tear down and a time build, a time to weep and a time laugh, a time to mourn and a time dance, a time to scatter stones and a time to gather them, a time to embrace and a time to refrain, a time to search and a time to give up, a time to keep and time to throw away, a time tear and a time to mend, a time to be silent and a time to speak, a time to love and a time to hate, a time for war and a time for peace." (**Ecclesiastes 3:1-8**).

It is good if we can be wise and learn how to communicate. Stick to the following words of wisdom and save your marriage:

- Pleasant words are a honeycomb, sweet to the soul and healing to the bones.

- "A gentle answer turns away wrath, but a harsh word stirs up anger" (**Proverbs 15:1**). Do not be harsh when talking to people. Be gentle to everybody even when people try to provoke you.

- "He who guards his lips guards his life, but he who speaks rashly will come to ruin" (**Proverbs 13:3**). It is better to keep quite than to talk too much.

- "Reckless words pierce like a sword, but the tongue of the wise brings healing" (**Proverbs 12:18**).When a wise person speaks, people get healed.

- We must not answer before we listen to what somebody wants to tell or ask us. The word of God tells us that "He who answers before listening- that is his folly and his shame" (**Proverbs 18:13**). Sometimes we allow anger to control us. When we are under the control of anger, we always answer before we could hear what somebody is about to tell us. God wants us to get rid of all those things that cause problems in our daily lives. **Ephesians 4:31** "Get rid of all bitterness, rage and anger, brawling and slander, along with every form of malice. Be kind and compassionate to one another, forgiving each other, just as in Christ God forgave you."

Bitterness, anger and hatred give birth to unforgiveness. Unforgiveness is a tool that the devil uses in different ways to different people. Married people, who cannot forgive each other, are dangerous to each other and to the society. The Bible teaches us to love one another. If we really love one another, unforgiveness will be lonely because it will not function.

-   We must learn to hold our tongues. There is an English proverb that says "speech is silver and silence is golden". It is better to keep quite than to talk too much. Talking too much can also make us sin.

- Women are advised not to be quarrelsome. Wise men think it is better to live on top of the roof that to live with a quarrelsome wife. **Proverbs 19:13** ".....a quarrelsome wife is like a constant dripping."

Women are taken as more talkative than men. Sometimes wives think that the way of solving things is to talk too much to their husbands. For them talking is closer to thinking out loud. The Bible tells us that what is impossible with man is possible with God. God is able to help us in controlling our tongue if we ask Him. **Matthew 19:26** "Jesus looked at them and said, 'With man this is impossible, but with God all things are possible."

Most of men do not talk too much. When they get upset, they prefer doing some kind of a job like clean the yard or doing the garden. Unlike women when they get upset, they talk too much. In most cases when husbands do not talk, wives are driven crazy. They think their husbands are not taking them serious and they end up including everybody in the house even children. In most families women have nick names that relate to the noise they make in their homes.

Wives must understand that in most cases husbands wants them to agree with them. If it comes to a point where the wife is not agreeing with her husband, the husband concludes by not talking to her any longer. The conversation will stop. Husband and wives are like two ships that sail together. For them to move together, one must reduce its speed to match that of the slower speed. In this case if a wife has been in high speed, she must reduce the speed to match her husband. This can only be achieved by asking from God.

In marriage, couples must strive towards the following:

- **Respect:** Good communication in marriage is respectful - The couples speak to each especially in front of people, they gain respect from others. People who are around will also respect what they are talking about. Humble and submissive wife is a treasure to her husband. The husband who loves his wife like the Jesus loves the church is honored by everybody. "A kindhearted woman gains respect......" (**Proverbs 11:16**).

- **Honesty/Integrity:** Good communication in marriage is honest – Honesty in marriage goes hand is hand with communication. Honest couples to each other communicate better than those who are not honest. In marriage, couples must not hide anything to each other. Hiding something from our spouses is a dangerous thing and this may lead to marital problems that may also lead to divorce.

God does not want His married children to be separated. "But at the beginning of creation God made them male and female. For this reason a man will leave his father and mother and be united to his wife, and the two will be become one flesh. So they are no longer two but one. Therefore what God has joined together, let man not separate" (**Mark 10:6-9**).

- **Capacity/Aptitude:** Good communication in marriage is of magnitude/capacity - In marriage communication must not be taken for granted. Couples must not let some of the things in the home to stay on their ways of communicating. Couples must not find it difficult to communicate. Communication in couples can take place while taking a walk, while working in the house, while watching television together, while holding family meetings, while driving to any places like to malls, to church or to any place you can decide to go to.

- **Enquiring/Search for more knowledge**: Communication in marriage enquire for more knowledge. Listening is important as it has been mentioned above. It is important in marriage to ask if one did not get what has been said well. Asking or enquiring in respectful manner may help the couples to gain trust in each other. Good knowledge is from God. God is the only one who reveals some of the things to us. If we need knowledge of how can we communicate with our spouses, let us ask God and we will get the answers.

- **Living in two way traffic**: Good communication in marriage is like two way traffic. The channel of traffic is not going in one where one would speak and the other one fails to listen. Speaking and listening is for two people. When one speaks, one must be a good listener so that the one who listens will answer in a correct manner respectfully. "Let the wise listen and add to their learning and let the discerning get the guidance" (**Proverbs 1:5**). Good communication in couples is when one admits to be corrected. "Whoever loves discipline loves knowledge but he who hates correction is stupid" (**Proverbs 12:1**).

"Drink the water from you own cistern, running water from your own well. Should your springs overflow in the streets, your streams of water in the public squares? Let them be yours alone, never to be shared with strangers. May your fountain be blessed and may you rejoice in the wife of your youth" (**Proverbs 5:15-18**). Do not harden your hearts. Turn to God; He is our Alfa and Omega.

Let us pray: Dear Heavenly Father, thank you for talking to me. Thank you for advising and teaching about simple things that causes damages to my marriage. Thank you that you still love me by showing me my mistakes. I am asking you in the Wonderful name of our Lord Jesus Christ to restore my marriage. I understand that marriage is blessed and ordained by you. I understand that we are joined by you and no man and no Devil should separate us. I thank you and I believe that my prayers are already answered by you because reconciliation is what you want from us. I promise to abide by your Word so that my marriage will be saved. I am asking these in Jesus Name - Amen

5. ARE YOU FACING DIVORCE?

You are not yet divorced – you are facing divorce. You are not in the final stage of divorce. It is not too late. Do not harden your heart. Holy Spirit is talking to you right now. You can make a U turn and face God.

These days divorce is a fat way of getting out of unpleasant marriage. Divorce is another painful stage in life that affects many people who relate with partners who want to divorce. Children are the first target in the divorce process before the final stage can be reached. Parents and relatives will also be affected. Divorce affects people spiritually, physically, financially and socially.

For marriage to be healthy and thriving, hardworking is needed from both husband and wife. Over a time things change in marriage. Those are relations, dreams and even people change. These changes are cause by things which were not there when you first meet each and decide in marriage.

For example; children were not there and you did not think that they would be stressful. You wanted children and you did not know that you would not have them. You did not plan to lose your job and some valuable things in marriage like job, house, car or even interest on your partner.

You loved each other so much that you did not expect your partner to have extra or an intimate relationship outside your marriage. Communication, sex problems and infidelity/ unfaithfulness are other problems that contribute in divorce.

In the book of **Malachi 2:16** "I hate divorce, says the Lord of Israel." Marriage is a lifetime commitment because the Bible teaches us that what God has joined together, let no man separate it." (**Matthew 19:6**).

God hates divorce but He does not hate you. God wants to teach us how to love the way He loves us. We must understand that in some cases divorce comes not because the partners wanted it or are happy about it. These words, "I hate divorce" are not coming from God because He wants to condemn us. It is because He has loves us.

You must understand that God values you more that He values your marriage. Try to work things out no matter how badly things can be. Put pride and selfishness aside. Consider each other as valuable creatures of God who created you in His image. I know there are stages where no one can stand like in the case where one is promised to be killed, where one is totally not prepared to compromise and where one is already hooked by the extra relationship with someone except his partner or vice versa.

If this will end up in divorce, that is where we say do not condemn yourself or push yourself hard. You are still the creation of God. He forgives and He hates divorce but He does not hate you.

Husbands and wives need to understand each other. Husbands need to understand how to handle their wives and this same applies to the wives. They must give their husbands the respect they need. Husbands must their wives with care. Wives need security in marriage and they need love, tenderness, protection appreciation, as it has been explained in the previous chapters. Husbands need to be providers, leaders, and protectors. The husband who feels needed and respected will also be less likely to divorce. Love is a choice and we must choose to love as God loved us.

God hates divorce because it courses people to commit sin of adultery. But God treats all sins alike as far as redemption is concerned. **John 8:4-11** "The teachers of the law and the

Pharisees brought in a woman caught in adultery. They made her stand before the group and said to Jesus, 'Teacher, this woman was caught in the act of adultery. In the Law Moses commanded us to stone such a woman. Now what do you say?' They were using this question as a trap in order to have a basis for accusing him. But Jesus bent down and started to write on the ground with his finger. When they kept on questioning him, He straightened up and said to them, "If any one of you is without sin, let him be the first one to throw a stone at her."

"Again he stopped down and wrote on the ground. At this, those who heard began to go away one at a time, the older ones fist, until only Jesus was left, with the woman still standing there. Jesus straightened up and asked her, 'woman, where are they? Has no one condemned you?" No on sir, she said. 'Then neither do I condemn you," Jesus declared. "**Go now and leave your life of sin**." In other translation it says "go and sin no more."

From these verses we can see that God treats all the sins alike. When God is calling us for repentance, He calls us all. He does not specify or categorize people with their sins. When He calls for all who are heavy loaded, he also calls them all not only specific people. If we turn to Jesus, no matter sin we committed, God will forgive us. In **Isaiah 1:18**, God is calling all of us with different sins. "Come now, let us reason together," says the Lord. "Though you sins are like scarlet, they shall be as white as snow; though they are red as crimson, they shall be like wool."

Forgiveness is for everybody not for certain people only. When God forgives us, He also promised us to remember our sins no more. **Hebrews 10:17** "Then he adds: Their sins and lawless acts, I will remember no more."

If God choose not to remember our sins why should we people remember our fellow brothers and sisters their sins. If God his children why should we not value our brothers and sisters. If people have repented from their sins of divorce, then in God's eyes their sins are gone and forgotten.

The compassion that Jesus had for people, the church also must have the same compassion for others. God hates divorce and He is not happy when His children part because of misunderstanding or any other issue. God wants to restore His children at all the times and He is ready to use any one who is willing.

Let us pray: Dear Heavenly Father, I ask you to help me to focus on my marriage so that it can grow and be better than it is today. Help me to put what I heard or read from this book in practice. Please give me the right attitude, help me to bare the fruit of the Spirit and remind me to give thanks on daily basis. Thank you for my partner and help me to respect him/ her all the times. I am asking these in Jesus Name. Amen.

6. IS YOUR PARTNER GIVING YOU HEADACHE?

Hebrews 3: 7-8 "So as the Holy Spirit says: '**Today**, if you hear His voice, do not harden your hearts as when they provoked me, as in the day of trial in the wilderness. Where your fathers tried me by testing me, and saw my works for forty years.'"

The partner who is giving headache is the partner who does not exist in your life. The partner who exists in your life is the partner who also has headache because you have headache. . "But at the beginning of creation God made them male and female. For this reason a man will leave his father and mother and be united to his wife, and the two will be become one flesh. So they are no longer two but one. Therefore what God has joined together, let man not separate" (**Mark 10:6-9**).

We are having headaches because we are separated. We separated what God said no one has to separate what God joined. God said the two shall become one flesh but unfortunately we separated that one flesh.

I was talking to one woman one time and she told me that her partner is giving her headache. She explained to me how she

67

cannot handle it anymore. The way she is tired, she feels like getting out their marriage. I was quite and listening attentively when she says all these negative things about her partner. After a while a look at her and say "may I ask you a simple question?" She said, yes you can ask me. I said "are you sure that you are not the one who is giving yourself a headache?" She said what do you mean? I said I mean are you sure you are not the one who is giving him a headache? She said, I do not understand you, and what do you mean? I said ok, are you sure that you have headache or is your partner who have headache caused by you.

In most cases partners blame each other that they have headache because of their partners whereas there is no headache but only misunderstanding between them. For one partner to keep quite whereas the other one is complaining does not mean that the partner who is quite does not have headache.

It is easy to avoid headaches in marriage. Jesus Christ said "I am the bread of life. He who com to me will never go hungry" (**John 6:35**). In marriages we have headaches because we are always in hunger of something. Jesus Christ says if we come to Him we will not go hungry.

John 8:12 "I am the light of the world. Whoever follows me will never walk in darkness." We have headaches because we are walking in the darkness. We are not following Jesus Christ. We are following our ways not the way of Jesus Christ.

"I am the gate; whoever enters through me will be saved" (**John 10:9**). In life there are many gates that people use to enter. Jesus is the only gate with guarantee of salvation.

"I am the good shepherd. The good shepherd lays down his life for the sheep" (**John 10:10**). It is important that we as sheep we know our shepherd who laid down His life for us.

John 11:25 "I am the resurrection and the life. He who believes in me will live, and even though he dies." Do not die because of headache believe in Jesus Christ and you will live.

I am the way, the truth and the life. No one comes to the Father except through me" (**John 14:6**). **Let us not neglect the way. Jesus Christ is our way and if we want to know the truth, He is the truth and the life.**

Do not harden you hearts. Holy Spirit is speaking with you today. Join what God joined to become one flesh. If there is forgiveness that is needed, ask for forgiveness. If it means getting rid of all those things that God does not want, get rid of them. **Ephesians 4:31** "Get rid of all bitterness, rage and anger, brawling and slander, along with every form of malice. Be kind and compassionate to one another, forgiving each other, just as in Christ God forgave you."

Go back to what attracted you to her and visa versa and the answer may be there. Life has a way of pulling people apart when it is the same routine day after day or you do not realize how fortunate you are to have each other. For the fact that you are married, it is a sign that you need each other. Think about it and start seeing things in a different eye.

In marriages headaches are caused by letter "I". We must always avoid using "I". In marriage "We" do things together to avoid headaches. We agree in good things together because we are not separated. We teach our children together. In all things we are together. There are some of the things that we get it so hard to do them together. Let us come to the real world. One good example is religion. Most of us we are Christians but we differ and the difference is caused by the different churches we are attending. This is one of the greatest causes of headache in partners. It is funny because we say that we serve one God with one Bible and gospel of Jesus Christ.

We must avoid being egocentric. Ego is another word that must be avoided. Selfishness in marriage destroys relationships. A selfish person does not care about others. A selfish person always forgets that there is other around him/her. A selfish partner always forget about his/her spouse. A selfish person does not love others like he/she loves he/ herself.

The word of God teaches us to love others as we love ourselves. This is the greatest commandment. "Love the Lord your God with all your heart and with all your soul and with your entire mind. This is the first and greatest commandment. And the second is like it Love your neighbor as yourself" (Matthew 22:37-39).

Let us pray: Dear Heavenly Father, I thank you for the suitable companion you gave to me. Help me to love my spouse the way you love me. Help me to be a good spouse and live the life that glorifies you. Help me to accept my spouse as you accepted me. Help me forgive him/her for whatever he/she did to me as your word teaches us to forgive those who did us wrong. I thank you that you are my Lord and you will never leave me nor forsake me. In Jesus Name I have prayed – Amen.

7. ARE YOUR CHILDREN TROUBLESOME?

When we say children are troublesome, what are we referring to? Do we mean drug addicts, stubborn, naughty or what type of children? Children are gifts from God. For the fact that, that child is born, it means there was a purpose. We miss this purpose because we fail to do some of the things that are required by God. When our children are misbehaving we become angry in such a way that we fail God somewhere.

Psalm 127:3-5 "Sons are heritage from the Lord, children are reward from him. Like arrows in the hands of a warrior are sons born in one's youth. Blessed is the man whose quiver is full of them. They will not be put to shame when they contend with their enemies in the gate."

When somebody buys you or gives you a gift, it means he knows more about the gift. When you do not understand how the gift operates, it is better to tell the person who bought that gift so that can refer you to where he bought it. Sometimes when our children are out of control, we try to put them in control whereas the own of the gifts is God.

In other instances we turn to God but we still hold on carrying the burden of our misbehaving children. The devil is too clever and he will always try to get us in many different ways. If the devil wants you to focus on him, he will get into your children knowing that you will lose control. The word of God tells to cast all the burdens to God for He cares. **1 Peter 5:7** "Cast all your anxiety on Him because He cares for you. Be self-control and alert. Your enemy the devil prowls around like a roaring lion looking for someone to devour."

To have misbehaving children is a heavy load that can lead to death. God wants us to throw all our heavy loads to Him. **Matthew 11:28-30** "Come to me, all you who are weary and burdened, and I will give you rest. Take my yoke upon and learn from me, for I am gentle and humble in heart and you will find rest for your souls for my yoke is easy and my burden is light."

Most of parents today are troubled by children who are drugs addict. Children are doing drugs at an early stage. Most of them cannot finish their high school studies because of drugs. This is a problem which is worldwide. Children who do drugs are burdens to parents and that we cannot run away from it. This is a worldwide problem.

The Bible teaches us that what is impossible with man it is possible with God. **Matthew 19:26** "With man this is impossible, but with God all things are possible." Parents, who are in trouble because of their children, may not understand what I am trying to say because the devil has blinded them by these problems of their children. "If you believe, everything is possible" (**Mark 9:23**). When the Bible tells us that all things are possible with God, it means even your drug addict child is not a problem to God to be solved. The Bible says "if you believe." You see, it is the matter of believing.

The problems you are facing, the situation you are in, the tough times you are going through were known by God before. God knew that you can handle them. Those tests will be testimonies one day.

Praying for troublesome children

Praying for our children is an ongoing process. We start praying for our children for the first time we realize that we are expecting them. We keep on praying for them until they are adults and so that they can also pray for their children. Even if they are adults, we do not stop praying for them. Prayer is communicating with God. We must communicate with our God – our Father on daily basis for us and for our children. We must pray without ceasing.

Living with troublesome children

Living with a troublesome child is a challenge. If a problematic child is yours, unfortunately you cannot switch or give him/her to somebody else. Crying every day or complaining about these children will never help. Instead you will suffer many sicknesses. Shake those problems off. When shaking them off, you will be lifted up.

Now it is the time. Let us get into the action. Do not harden your heart because Holy Spirit is talking to you today.

Remember the day you gave birth to that child. God gave you that child with love. Do not hold on him even if he is hurting you. Surrender that child to his creator. Let the creator panel beat him. It was not by mistake that God gave you that child.
The name you gave that child must have meant something to you.

Turn everything that devil is making worst to best. Think of yourself and how many times did God call you for repentance or to turn away from anything that God does not wants. It took you a long time until you respond to the calling of God. Maybe even today you have not yet responded to the calling of God. But God did not give up on you. So please do not give up on that child.

God has been patient with you; it is now the time for you to be patient with you child. God is showing you love every day, please show love to your child on daily basis. Train your children, discipline them where necessary and tell them about good news of God.

God is going to answer you at His time not at your time. God is either training you or your children. Receive the training so that you can have good results.

"Train a child the way he should go and when he is old he will not turn from it" (**Proverbs 22:6).** We must not be scared to discipline our children as God also discipline us.

Let us pray: My dear Lord Jesus Christ thank you for the children you gave me. Help me to love and teach them your ways on daily basis. Help me to be a good parent that lead by a good example to my children. Forgive them for everything they are doing which are not good before your eyes. Protect them wherever they are and guide them to whatever they do. Anoint them with fresh anointing on daily basis. Help them to live their lives for you and let their lives glorify you on daily basis. Help them to forgive those who did them wrong and lead them not into the temptations. For thine is the Kingdom, the power and the glory forever and ever. I ask these in Jesus Name – Amen.

8. ARE YOU REJECTED?

Rejection is one of the most painful situations in life that one has to face one way or the other. Dealing with rejection and getting the past hurt is not easy but it can be done. It is not easy to stand up from the ground and move on as if nothing had happened. But with the help of God we can. God knows all our situations and He will never leave us nor forsake us.

Rejection hurts but you need to face it, to fix it and move on. It is of no use to keep on hiding in your house. Avoiding people or drinking liquor with the aim of taking off the problem. Face the reality and deal with the pain. Socialize with good people share good news with others; listen to others who have been rejected and learn how they cope with rejection. Accept yourself to be accepted.

Before you think of being rejected you must consider this: **Proverbs 17:22** "A cheerful heart is a good medicine but a crushed spirit dries up the bones." Do not think that you are the only one who is rejected. Mostly everybody was rejected somehow.

God created us with love. Everything that is created with love is to be loved and accepted by everybody. God accepts us all as He created us and we are to accept each other as we are. Rejection may come from many sources. Fear is one of them and fear is the opposite of faith.

1 John 4:18 "There is no fear in love. But perfect love drives out fear, because fear has to do with punishment. The one who fears is not made perfect in love." Many people liked to be loved and being popular. Rejection can stop us to move forward with life.

If rejection is a curse then confidence is the cure. The way to fix rejection is to balance it with confidence by investing in fun activities and positive thinking. It is important to feel good about yourself. No one will come from another place to feel good for you. God created you with purpose and you must be confident enough to do what God created you to do. The more confident you are, the better you will be able to cope with most forms of rejection.

Dealing with rejection

- **Do not take rejection personally:** Not being taken into the consideration, not being loved or not being accepted does not mean that you are worthless. For the fact that you are alive, it means that you worth more. It is important to learn that not everything is about you. God prepares His people for all the situation that suit them. Sometimes we want things that will not be good for us in future. God is Omniscience. When something is not happening the way you want it, it means God is protecting you from being hurt in future.

- **Be prepared to start afresh when things did no go well:** Face rejection and refuse to let your past disappointments discolor your present opportunities. The word of God teaches us that in everything God works for the good of those who love Him. **Romans 8:28** "And we know that in all things God works for the good of those who love Him."

- **Honesty pays:** It is important to be honest of what makes you feel rejected. Sometimes people know it very well that they are rejected because of something but they mentioned something else. For an example one may feel rejected because he did not occupy better position at work or at any place where he expected to be given the position but when the problem has to be addressed, he mentioned something else.

It is good if you feel being rejected because you were not promoted at, say it as it is. Tell people that you feel rejected because you were not promoted. The advice is, accept the situation and try again.

- **Giving up in life is a sign of accepting rejection:** Do not capitalize on rejection, rather accept failure and try again. Allow people to help you and be positive. There is no pain that last forever.

Dealing with rejection in relationship

Many people think that rejection in marriage is worse than any other rejection. That is not true, rejection is rejection. In this part we are going to deal with rejection in relationship or in marriage. Once you are dumped, there are stages you have to face. In facing those stage, you must not forget that what is impossible with men it is possible with God. God is always available in the worst situation where nothing is expected.

- **There is this stage of denial.** Do not let yourself in the situation where you are blaming yourself because you are dumped. Accept that you are dumped and focus on our Creator. The problem is; in many things we forget to focus on God. God wants us to depend on Him in everything.

There is a time where we forget about God and we concentrate on our affairs. We concentrate on the relationship but we forget the creator of the relationship. We concentrate on the blessings we forget the Blesser. Happy relationship is a blessing from God. When God bless us with a partner who makes you happy at all the times, you must always give thanks to God. "Be joyful always, pray continually, give thanks in all circumstance, for this is God's will for you in Christ Jesus" (**1 Thessalonians 5:16-18**).

Do not harden your heart, shake it off and go back and check where you lost it. It is not too late. If forgiveness is needed, do not hesitate, ask for it and you must also be forgiving. If we do not forgive those who did us wrong, our Father will not forgive us. To keep on denying that you are dumped is the wasting of time. If you take yourself as the poor dumped somebody, God is looking at you like His child who needs Him as the Father. No father will let his child not to be happy. Our Father in heaven wants us to be happy all the times.

- There is this stage where one starts to think of many things that may have caused the rejection. Stop driving yourself crazy by thinking of all those things that you think they contributed on the rejection. Stop taking rejection personal. Do not try to change who you are in order to impress the partner who dumped you. You are the way you are because God created you like that. God loves you and there is a lot that God has for you.

Learn to move on and turn the rejection into acceptance. There are people who will accept you the way or who you are.

Do not be angry or develop hatred because these will cause you not to forgive the person who dumped you. **Ephesians 4:31** "Get rid of all bitterness, rage and anger, brawling and slander, along with every form of malice. Be kind and compassionate to one another, forgiving each other, just as in Christ God forgave you."

No matter the type of rejection you are suffering, there is an end to the pain. Do not focus on the pain but rather on the end of pain and hurt. If you focus on the rejection, you must know that you strengthen the pain. Everything has the starting time and the ending time. "There is time to weep and time to laugh" (**Ecclesiastes 3:4**).

We must ask God to search our hearts and make us clean. **Psalm 66:18-20** "If I had cherished sin in my heart, the Lord would not have listened; but God has surely listened and heard my voice in prayer. Praise God who has not rejected my prayer or withheld his love from me." **Psalm 139:23** "Search me, O God, and know my heart; test me and know my anxious thoughts."

Let me tell you something that you are not aware of – "God is your Creator and you look beautiful. Accept yourself as the chosen one of God." **Proverbs 15:30** "A cheerful look brings joy to the heart, and good news gives health to the bones." Many people and opportunities are waiting for you outside and you are wasting time by rejecting yourself.

Accept yourself and help us to accept you. We want to accept you but you are a stumbling block because of that negative attitude. You are the right vessel to be used by God and you are delaying God to use you.

Let us pray: Dear Heavenly Father, I thank you for your Word that says "Therefore, if anyone is in Christ, he is a new creation; the old has gone, the new has come." I thank you that I am your new creation. I thank you for the love you have been showing me since I was born even if I was not aware. I thank you for opening my spiritual eyes to see all good things. I thank you for opening my spiritual ears to hear all good things about me and you my Father. Help me to forgive all those who rejected me and help me to love them they way you loved me. Forgive me also for rejecting myself and help me to live a new life that glorifies you with everything I do. Help me to live my life for you alone and I ask these in Jesus Name – Amen.

9. DO NOT GIVE UP ON GOD

Do not listen to the deceiving words of the Devil that God does not exist or God will never give you the desires of your heart. "Do not fret because of evil men or be envious of those who do wrong. For like the grass they will soon whither, like green plants they will soon die away. Trust in the Lord and do good; dwell in the land and enjoy safe pasture. Delight yourself in the Lord and he will give you the desires of your heart" (**Psalm 37:1-4**). The Word of God teaches us that if we delight in the Lord, He will give us the desires of our hearts. No matter what we desire, the Lord will give us. If the promise is like this, it means we need not worry about anything. Whatever we desire, God will give it to us.

In life we come across different situations where we end up not knowing what to believe. We desire this and that and we end up not believing that God will give us what we desire. As Christians we must know that every situation comes to us because God exists and God is for us. Apostle Paul said in the book of Romans that "If God is for us, who can be against us" (**Romans 8:31**). Do not be discouraged, "Be on your guard; stand firm in the faith; be men of courage; be strong" (**1**

Corinthians 16:13). God proved to many nations in the Old Testament that He is alive and He is the only God.

In book of Exodus, God is giving us this law that we must not have any other god than Him. This means that if God is jealous for us to have other gods, He will not leave us nor forsake. He will not give up on us if we are doing what is right before His eyes. **Exodus 20:2- 6** "I am the Lord your God, who brought you out of Egypt, out of the land of slavery. You shall have no other gods before me. You shall not make for yourself an idol in the form of anything in heaven above or on the earth beneath or in the waters below. You shall not bow down to them or worship them; for I , the Lord your God, am a jealous God, punishing the children for the sin of the fathers to the third and fourth generation of those who hate me, but showing love to a thousand generations of those who love me and keep my commandments."

In the book of 2 Kings 5; Naaman was healed leprosy because an Israelite slave girl told him about the man of God who was in Samaria. **2 Kings 5:2** "Now bands from Aram had gone out and had taken captive a young girl from Israel and she served Naaman's wife". This girl was kept in captive and one can imagine how life was in her side. I think everything was not good. She could have given up on God because she was taken from her country. Instead she advised her mistress that if only her master would see the prophet who is in Samaria' he would cure him of his leprosy. **2 Kings 5:3** "She said to her mistress, 'if only my master would see the prophet who is in Samaria! He would cure him of his leprosy."

Naaman was the commander of the army of the king of Aram. He was a great man in the sight of his master and highly regarded, because through him the Lord had given victory to Aram but he had leprosy. This book of 2 Kings Chapter 5, is teaching us not to be discouraged. The girl was not discouraged that she is in captive, she was not angry for God because of what happened to her and she told her mistress about the man of God who can help her master.

Naaman did not hesitate, he went to Samaria but he was disappoint that the man of God did not tough him or even come to meet him as he knew that he was a great commander. In verse 9-11, "So Naaman went with his horses and chariots and stopped at the door of Elisha's house. Elisha sent a messenger to say to him, 'go wash yourself seven times in the Jordan, and your flesh will be restored and you will be cleansed.' Namaan did not belief and he went away angry and said, 'I thought that he would surely come out to me and stand and call on the name of the Lord his God, wave his hand over the spot and cure me of my leprosy."

There is a serious problem in here. Namaan, because of his status did not belief that someone will talk to him in the way the man of God talked to him. He wanted man of God to come out and see him or even touch him. God wanted to show Namaan that He is a great God. He does not care about the status of any person but He cares about the person as he is. The servants of Naaman talked to him to do what the prophet of God was telling him. **2 Kings 5:13-14** "Namaan servant went to him and said, 'My father, if the prophet had told you to do some great thing, would you not have done it? How much more, then, when he tells you, 'wash and be cleansed'!" So he went down and dipped himself in the Jordan seven times, as the man of God had told him, and his flesh was restored and became clean like that of a young boy."

I like this verse where Namaan belief that there is not God in the whole world. Verse 14 **"Then Namaan and all his attendants went back to the man of God. He stood before**

him and said, "Now I know that there is no God in the entire world except in Israel." The slave girl did not give up on God and God used her in that painful situation to let people know that there is no other God than God in Israel. Namaan was ill and his illness drove him closer to God.

You might be in any situation where you are discouraged and you feel that God does not love you. Some people end up questioning the love of God. They end up blaming God for their circumstances. No matter what situation you are in, God loves you and God wants to us in that situation to show people that He is alive and Omnipresent. He knows everything – He is Omniscience.

It is good to make positive impact to other people. God heals the brokenhearted and binds up their wounds. Great is our Lord and mighty in power; his understanding has no limit. Do not give up on God. God wants to use you because you have the ability to make an impact that will never be erased. You have the gifts to impact to others and help them to stand taller, become stronger and better equipped to handle the struggles and trials of life.

The Bible declares in **Galatians 6:9-10** "Let us not become weary in doing good, for at the proper time we will reap a harvest if we do not give up. Therefore, as we have opportunity, let us do well to all people, especially to those who belong to the family of believers."

In book of Acts chapter 16, God used the situation of Paul and Silas to save the jailer and his family. Before they could be thrown into the jail, they were stripped and beaten. "When the owners of the slave girl realize that their hope of making money was gone, they seized Paul and Silas and dragged them into the marketplace to face the authorities. They brought them before the magistrates and said, 'these man are Jews, and are throwing our city into an uproar by advocating customs unlawful for us Romans to accept or practice.

The crowd joined in the attack against Paul and Silas and the magistrates ordered them to be stripped and beaten. After they had been severely flogged, they were thrown into prison and jailer was commanded to guard them carefully. Upon receiving such orders, he put them in the inner cell and fastened their feet in the stocks" (**Acts 16: 19-24**).

This was the time which Paul and Silas could have given up on God because they were stripped and beaten whilst delivering the message of God. They were so severely ill-treated in the front of God because God is Omnipresent. They were taken to the place where it is known as the place for criminals, the place where everybody think that the children of God do not belong. They were in the situation where everybody think that servant of God cannot be. But they did not give up on God.

If you are a servant of God, God will send to any place where He wants to save His children. The jailer did not know that, that day was the day for him and his family to be delivered or to be saved. "Upon receiving such orders, he put them in the inner cell and fastened their feet in the stocks" (**Act 16:24**). The jailer was following the orders of the magistrates and he also wanted his name to be good. He did not know that it was his day and Paul and Silas did not know that God send them there by purpose.

There is a purpose in each and every situation you get in. "About midnight Paul and Silas were praising and singing hymns to God, and the other prisoners were listening to them" (**Acts 16:25**). They were listening to them and at the same time they were amazed that really can somebody praise God who did not help him when he was thrown in the jail. I think other prisoners wanted to mock them for their foolishness but God close their mouth because God was on operation.

God wanted to show other prisoners and jailer that there is nothing that is hard to Him. What is impossible with men, it is possible with God. Suddenly something miraculous happened. By praise and worship, God shook the big building of jail. **Act 16:26-** "Suddenly there was such a violent earthquake that the foundations of the prison were shaken. At once all the prison doors flew open **and everybody's chains came to lose.**" When you are in prison, it means you are in bondage. To be out of bondage you must be delivered. Paul and Silas were thrown in jail not knowing that it was the plan of God for them to release prisoners, to set the captive free. The book of **Isaiah 61:**1 teaches us that "The Spirit of the Lord is upon me, because the Lord has anointed me to preach the good news to the poor. He has sent me to bind up the broken heart, to proclaim freedom for the captive and to release from darkness for the prisoners."

The Spirit of the Lord was upon Paul and Silas and again the Spirit of the Lord is upon us. The problems you are encountering now or the situations you are going through is because the Spirit of the Lord is upon you and you must release the captive. It will not help you to give up on God and concentrate on your problems. Concentrating on the problems or the situations will not help you. Instead you are going to see it growing bigger and bigger day by day. It is important to see how big is our God rather than seeing how big our problems are.

"When the jailer woke up, and he saw the prison doors open and when he saw the prison doors open, he drew his sword and was about to kill himself because he thought the prisoners has escaped. But Paul shouted, 'Don't harm yourself! We are all here!'" (**Acts 16:27-28**). The Bible tells us 'the jailer woke up.' Sometimes when life run smooth for us we sleep and we forget God. We think we do not need Him because we are ok with everything. In this sense we did not gave up on God but we forgot about him.

God will wake you up in different ways. The jailer was frightened by the earthquake that shook the foundations of prison which cause the doors to be opened. Because it was the plan of God, nobody ran away after everybody's chains came loose. The plan of God was for the trials and tribulations of Paul and Silas to set the captive free. The problems you are encountering now are for somebody to be free. They are for somebody to receive his /her deliverance.

Do not give up on God because you do not know His plans for you. "The jailer called for lights, rushed in and fell trembling before Paul and Silas. He them brought them out and asked, Sirs, what must I do to be saved?" They replied, Believe in the Lord Jesus, and you will be saved – you and your household," then they spoke the word of the Lord to him and to all the others in his house. At that hour of the night the jailer took them and washed their wounds; then immediately he and all his family were baptized. The jailer brought them into his house and set a meal before them; he was filled with joy because he had come to believe on God – he and his whole family" (**Act 16:29-34**).

The painful situation of Paul and Silas make an impact on the life of the jailer and his family. Their situation brought life to the jailer because they did not give up on God. No matter the trials and tribulations that we go through in life, we should always stay in faith and remember that God has us securely in the palms of Hid Hands. No matter how hard the enemy tries to discourage your heart, remind yourself that you are well able to withstand and triumph over every attack that the enemy can bring. The Lord gives strength; faith and a quiet confidence letting us know that we can overcome every trial that comes our way. We just have to rest in His promise knowing that if God brought us to it, He will also bring us through it. When we pass through that trial, we will be made stronger, wiser and better able to handle more of life's challenges down the road.

Every obstacle serves a purpose to teach us lessons, to show us our inner strength, to build our confidence in God and to remind us that nothing is impossible to those who believe. Always remember the love of the Lord to you when the times of doubt knock at your door. God believe in you and you must always believe in yourself. With God, impossible means nothing. Raise your confidence in him and let God know that your eyes will continue to stay focused on the One who is Great.

"Therefore, since we are surrounded by such a great cloud of witness, let us throw off everything that hinders and the sin that so easily entangles, and let us run with perseverance the race marked out for us. Let us fix our eyes on Jesus, the author and perfecter of our faith, who for the joy set before him endured the cross, scorning its shame, and sat down at the right hand of the throne of God" **(Hebrews 12:1-2**).

God loves us as His sons and the father who loves his children always disciplines them. **Hebrews 12:5-7** ".....My sons, do not make light of the Lord's discipline, and do not lose heart when he rebukes you, because the Lord disciplines those he loves, and he punishes everyone he accepts as a son. Endure hardships as discipline; God is treating you as sons."

Waiting patiently and allowing God to work in our lives will benefit us a lot. The Bible teaches us about Job who lost everything he accumulated on earth. But everything was restored after he prayed for his friends who were advising him to give up on God.

Job 42:10 "After Job prayed for his friends, the Lord made him prosperous again and gave him twice as much as he had before." Job was heavy loaded with troubles, he was sick, his wife and his friends advise him to give up on God, he used to pray for his children whilst they were not with him because he understood that they may be doing what was not good before the Lord. Apart from all these he waited patiently upon the Lord to come up with good answer and he benefited.

Job was patient and he inherited God promise. If we wait patiently we will enjoy the fruit of the spirit. Our character will be perfect if we are patient. **James 1:4** "Let patience have its perfect work, that you may be perfect and complete."

James 5:10-11 "Be patient, then brothers, until the Lord's coming. See how the farmer waits for the land to yield its valuable crop and how patient he is for the autumn and spring rains. You too, be patient and stand firm, because the Lord's coming is near."

We must learn to ride flow with the patience of the Holy Spirit in our daily lives and to walk with the Lord – and we will then be able to enter into a much more restful and peaceful state of mind and emotion.

We must not think that God is slow in doing things or in answering our prayers. God wants everybody to repent. He does not want anybody to perish. **2 Peter 3:9** "The Lord is not slow in keeping His promise, as some understand slowness. He is patient with you, not wanting anyone to perish, but wants everyone to come to repentance,"

Let us pray: Dear Lord Jesus Christ, I thank you for being with me through all these trial and tribulations. Thank you for your guidance and protection. I know that you have been with me through all these hard times and I want to thank you once more for not forsaking me as you promised in your Word that you will never leave me nor forsake me. I now know that you do not want anybody to perish and it is for us to understand your patience and learn from you. I will praise you all the times and I thank you for everything in Jesus Name - Amen.

10.   OVERCOME THE DEVIL

The devil who is in the supernatural realm will never give up on you. He will always try to get. He will try all means when trying to get children of God. It is important that we know who we are in Christ. He will always try by everything mentioned above and even others which are not mentioned in this book. He will try you by sicknesses, troublesome children, spouse that gives headache and also marriage that is not healthy.

The devil and his tricks have no power on us. The Bible tells us in the book of **1 John 4:4** "But you belong to God, my children and have defeated the false prophets, because the Spirit who is in you is more powerful than the spirit in those who belong to the world."

There is no way, the devil can overcome us. What the devil is afraid of the most is the blood of Lord Jesus Christ. By sheddig of His blood, the Lord crushed the head of the devil. The power and authority were given to us by our Lord Jesus Christ. Jesus Christ told us in the book of **Luke 10:18-19** that he saw devil fall like lightening from heaven. Jesus answered them "I saw Satan fall like lightning from heaven. Listen! I have given you authority, so that you can walk on snakes and scorpions and overcome all the power of the Enemy and nothing will hurt you."

Through the blood of our Lord Jesus Christ, Satan was destroyed. Jesus Christ destroyed him on our behalf. There is no need for us to be worried about something that was defeated long time ago. God gave us the authority to control the devil not the devil to control us. We must know that he is under our feet. "Since the children have flesh and blood, he too shared in their humanity so that by his death he might destroy him who hold the power of death that is the devil" (**Hebrews 2"14**).
'

If the saints continually trust in the precious blood of the Lord and take the stand of **Romans 6:11-13**, Satan will be defeated as Jesus has already defeated him on the Cross by the blood. "In the same way, count yourself dead to sin but alive to God in Christ Jesus. Therefore do not let sin reign in your mortal body so that you obey its evil desire. Do not offer the parts of your body to sin, as instruments of wickedness, but rather offer yourselves to God, as those who have been brought from death to life, and offer the parts of your body to him as instruments of righteousness." Christians are often attacked and accused by the Devil because they have given ground to sin and this has afforded the enemy the opportunity to accuse them. If we can understand the above scripture; **Roman 6:11-13,** we will not offer our parts of body to sin. The Devil base his attacks on us through the sins we commit.

The Word of God teaches us that we overcame because of the blood. We must thank God because His blood does not only save us but it also enables us to be victorious in our Christians life. All of our victories come because of the blood, **Revelation 12:11** "They overcame him [Devil] by the blood of the Lamb and by the word of their testimony." We overcome by speaking the Word of God. His Word is a double edged sword. We need to know the Word and we also need to understand that it takes the blood and the Word to overcome. The Word of God teaches us in **John 8:31-32** "If you abide in My Word, you are my disciples indeed. And you shall know the truth and the truth shall set you free." Sin has no dominion over us as the Devil is already been defeated. As is has been explained above that the Devil does not give up, believers should always be alert because this will not stop him from accusing us not attacking us.

Christians must continuously hide under the blood of Jesus Christ to avoid attacks of the devil. Christians must live by the Word of God. The Bible tells us that we are strong and the word of God lives in us. "Because you are strong and the Word of god live in you and you have overcome the evil one" (**1 John 2:14**). Because of His Word that is in us, we overcame the Devil but the problem is that Christians are not aware.

Hebrews 4:12 "For the Word of God is living and active. Sharper than any double edged sword, it penetrates even to dividing soul and spirit, joint and marrow, it judges the thoughts an attitudes of the heart." God's Word is powerful and alive. It is operative and we must trust Him [God] for His protection. We must let the Word of God dwell in us and fill our hearts and by this, the Devil will always loose the battle.

We must submit ourselves to God and resist the Devil. We cannot submit two leaders. If we submit to the one who is good, the bad one will run away because we will be resisting him. The Bible tells us in **James 4:7-8** "Submit yourselves, then to God. Resist the Devil and he will flee from you. Come near God and He will come near you…"

The command from the above verse is submit to God. You do not submit to God and allow the Devil to play next to you. You submit to God and resist the Devil. If you resist the Devil, he will not stay next to you and wait to see what will happen next. The Bible tells us that we must resist him and he will fly from us.

When we resist the Devil, we must exercise our will. We must tell him that he is not allowed in our lives or in hearts. We must tell him that he does not have rights in our lives. In the book of Understanding the tool of the Devil, I explained about the rights of the Devil. The Devil will not leave if you do not do away with his rights and exercise your will by telling him that he does not have right to stay next to you. If you know your story, the Devil will not stay next to you. He will try at all the times but he will fail because you will be exercising your will. By telling him that "In the Name of our Lord and Savior Jesus Christ who has overcome you; I will not allow you next to me and I resist you."

After telling him these words, we must have faith that based on God's Word, the devil ran away. We must praise and thank God that we are free. We must not allow him or his accusations that we are not free from him. If we practice our faith, the Devil will not stay in us. Jesus Christ conquered the Devil by telling him that it is written in the Word of God that....... We must also tell him that it is written that "Greater is He that is in us than the one who is on earth." Christians must be able to rebuke the Devil immediately when they realize that he (Devil) is opening the mouth to say something to them. They must not give him a chance by listening first and try to rebuke after. We should not listen to him because by giving him our ears, we will be giving a chance to convince us to fall for his tricks.

The Devil is full of tricks and to give him a little chance, it will be our downfall. The Bible teaches us that we must not give the Devil a foothold or an opportunity for reproach. **Ephesians 4:27** "and do not give a Devil a Foothold." We must not allow the Devil to use us as his factory to manufacture his production of sin.

Little evil things we allow in our lives will end up in big uncontrollable sins. One man was traveling from place to another. As he was on his way; he saw the snake under the big stone which it could not pushed away. The snake was there waiting for someone to come and roll the stone away so that it can push its mission.

People passed there but they did not give the snake the chance of listening to it as they knew that the snake is a Devil. But this man gave the snake a chance of listening when it talks to him. The snake requests the man to roll the big stone that was pressing the snake down so that it can be free. The man knew that the snake will bite him but he believe the snake when it tells him that it could not do such an evil thing.

The Devil is evil; there is no way he can do good things. This man removes the stone on top of the snake and immediately the snake shows the man its colors and promise to bite him. The man was in trouble until one clever man came and asked what the problem was. The man explained everything to the stranger and the stranger reversed everything.

The stranger asked the snake to lay the way it laid on the ground and the snake did. Stranger asked the man to put the stone on top of the snake the way it was and the man did. Now the stranger told the man that "you see now; the snake is a Devil and it belongs under the stone. So as the Devil, he belongs under our feet. We must not listen to him." If we listen to him, he will control and destroy us.

We must try to be stable. Our yes must be yes and our no must be no. The Devil always capitalize on our doubts or our fear. He knows very well that fear is the opposite of faith. We must allow Holy Spirit to dwell in us so that the Devil will not have a chance. The authority over the power of the enemy has been given to us by our Lord Jesus Christ. We get this in **Luke 10:18-19**. Even how powerful the enemy can be, our Lord gave us the authority to suppress the enemy. We must not doubt this authority. The enemy's power cannot prevail against the authority from the Lord.

Let us pray: Dear Heavenly Father thank you for the authority you gave us. Thank you for defeating the Devil for us on the cross and thank you again for the precious blood that cleansed us for our inequities. Thank you for your Word that make us strong every day. I thank you as your Word teaches us to give thanks on everything. In Jesus Name I have prayed. Amen.

11.   YOU HAVE ALL THE ANSWERS

After reading about all these, you have all the answers. Do not harden your heart because the Spirit of the Lord is speaking to you right now.

Are you heavy loaded? "Come to me you all who are weary and burdened, and I will give you rest. Take my yoke upon and learn from me, I am gentle and humble in heart and you will find rest for your souls for my yoke is easy and my burden is light." (**Matthew 11:28-30**). Heavy loads in life are not for us but our Lord is prepared to carry them for us so that we can be free and be free in deed.

Are your sick? Jesus Christ is our Healer, our Jehovah Rapha, and the Lord who heals. If we call on the Name of our Lord Jesus Christ, we know that we get everything we need; healing, forgiveness, peace, divine protection and we are also saved. **Isaiah 53:5** "But He (Jesus) was pierced for our transgressions, He was crushed for our iniquities; the punishment that brought us peace was upon Him, and by His wounds we are **healed.**"

Is your marriage going down the drain? God has ordained and blessed marriage. "The Lord God said, it is not good that man should be alone; I will make him a helper suitable for him" (**Genesis 2:18**). From the beginning God said "it is not good for a man to be alone." And He made him a suitable helper. The wife or the husband you are staying with is suitably made for you. It is not a mistake. God will never lie. He is not a man that He should lie or a son of a man that He should change His mind.

Healthy marriages require **time, attention, energy and vigilance/ care**. It needs effort to have super marriage. Do not run marriage like a business. Marriage is of God and He is the one who can service it better that anyone else.

Are facing divorce? You are not yet divorced – you are facing divorce. You are not in the final stage of divorce. It is not too late. Do not harden your heart. Holy Spirit is talking to you right now. You can make a U turn and face God. "What is impossible with man, it is possible with God" (**Luke 18:27).**

Is your partner giving you a headache? We are having headaches because we are separated. We separated what God said no one has to separate what God joined. God said the two shall become one flesh but unfortunately we separated that one flesh.

"But at the beginning of creation God made them male and female. For this reason a man will leave his father and mother and be united to his wife, and the two will be become one flesh. So they are no longer two but one. Therefore what God has joined together, let man not separate" (**Mark 10:6-9**).

Are your children troublesome? Children are gifts from God. For the fact that child is born, it means there was a purpose. We miss this purpose because we fail to do some of the things that are required by God. When our children are misbehaving we become angry in such a way that we fail God somewhere. We must surrender all to God including our children. We cannot put our children on the right way, only God can do that for us. We must seek the kingdom of God and the rest shall follow. All other things will be added unto us.

Are you rejected? Rejection is one of the most painful situations in life that one has to face one way or the other. Dealing with rejection and getting past the hurt is not easy but it can be done. It is not easy to stand up from the ground and move on as if nothing had happened. But with the help of God we can. God knows all our situations and He will never leave us nor forsake us.

Have courage and patience for the great sorrows of life. Patience is not a desperate waiting in doubt, but a hopeful waiting in confidence. Patience with God is faith and with other is love. When we patiently wait for the Lord through persecution, pain, depression, boredom and troublesome circumstances, we may unknowingly lead others to Christ.

Our Lord was persecuted but He did not give up on the one who send Him. Patience is the best remedy for every trouble. It make us good example for others who are looking at us. People can learn everything good from us through patience.

Let us pray: Precious Lord Jesus Christ, I thank you for you are always there for me. I thank you for answering my prayers and showing me who I am in your Kingdom. I thank you for bringing your servant to my side to help me with all I needed during my trial and tribulations. Thank you for the strength you gave me as your Word says "let the sick say I am healed and let the weak say I am strong. I confess that I can do everything with Christ who strengthens me. I speak prophetically that, my marriage is in order, I am healed, my children are alright, my spouse is on the right track and my Lord is my shepherd and I shall not want. I thank you because you prepare a table before me in the presence of my enemies and surely the goodness and love will follow me all the day of my life and I will dwell in the house of the Lord forever and in Jesus Name I have prayed. Amen.

12.   CONCLUSION

Do not harden your heart. God is with you. He will never leave you nor forsake you. Do not disown God because He will disown you. **2 Timothy 2:11-12** "Here is the trustworthy saying. If we died with Him, we will also live with Him. If we endure, we will also reign with Him. If we disown Him, He will disown us, if we are faithless, He will remain faithful for He cannot disown Himself."

Believe in yourself with deepest of heart and the ultimate grace of God. Avoid following the acts of sins and begin to love others with purity. Be spiritual and not physical and plan your works to bring stability in your mind so that you may concentrate in the praise, worships and prayers of God.

Do not let your today to be over before you decide. Do not harden your heart because hardening the heart is not only time wasting but also dangerous as we do not know what will happen tomorrow.

- Come to Jesus for your heavy load, **(Matthew 11:28-30).**
- Believe in the Lord for your healing, **(Isaiah 53:5).**

- Husbands love your wives and wives be submissive to you husbands, **(Ephesians 5:22, 25, 28).**
- Do not let divorce condemn you, God forgives, **(Hebrews 10:17).**
- Love your partner as you love yourself, (Matthew 22:37-39).
- Love your children; they are gifts from God, **(Psalm 127:3-5).**
- Love and forgive others to overcome the spirit of rejection. Love covers everything, (1 Corinthians 13).
- Do not give up on God; He will give you the desires of your heart, **(Psalm 37:1-4).**
- After all these the Devil is defeated, **(Revelation 12:11).**
- Dear friends, do not be surprised at the painful trial you are suffering, as though something strange were happening to you. But rejoice that you participate in the sufferings of Christ, so that you may be over-joyed when his glory is revealed. **(1 Peter 4:12-13).**
- Jesus is the answer, surrender to Him, give your life to Him and He will take care of you. Amen.

Let us pray: Precious Lord Jesus Christ thank you for being with me through this journey. I understand that you are the answer to all my problems and I re-dedicate my life to you. Thank you for your love and help me to love everybody the way you love me. Thank you for teaching me through this book and I repent from all sins I committed. I ask you to help me live better life so that I can lead others to you. I ask all these in the Name of our Lord Jesus Christ – Amen.

Biblical References

1. Genesis 2:17 & 18
2. Exodus 15:26, 20:2-6
3. Numbers 23:19
4. 2 Kings 5:2 & 3, 5:13-14 & 7:3-4
5. Job 42:10
6. Psalm 37:1-4, 55:22, 68:19, 103:2-3 & 127:3-5
7. Proverbs 1:5, 5:15-18 & 19
8. Proverbs 11:16
9. Proverbs 12:1, 4, 15:1, 18:13 &22
10. Proverbs 19:13 & 22:6
11. Ecclesiastes 3:1-8, 3:4
12. Isaiah 1:18, 40:29-3, 53:5 & 61:1-3
13. Jeremiah 29:11-13
14. Ezekiel 36:26
15. Malachi 2:16, 3:6
16. Matthew 6:5-29 & 33, 7:7-8, 11:28-30
17. Matthew 19:6 & 26
18. Mark 9:23, 10:6-9
19. Luke 10:38-42
20. John 1:1-3, 6:35, 8:4-11& 12, 8:31-32,
21. John 10:9 & 10, 11:25,
22. John 14:6 & 13 -15 & 18,15:1
23. Acts 16: 19-24 & 15, 16:27-28
24. Romans 6:11-13 & 8:28, 31
25. 1 Corinthians 7:3-4, 11:8-9, 13:4-8 & 13,

26.   1 Corinthians 16:13
27.   Galatians 6:9-10
28.   Ephesians 4:29-32, 4:31, 5:22-23,
   5:25
29.   Ephesians 5:25 & 28
30.   Philippians 4:6
31.   Colossians 3:13
32.   Colossians 3: 18 & 19
33.   1 Thessalonians 5:16-18
34.   2 Timothy 2:11-12
35.   Hebrews 2"14
36.   Hebrews 12:1-2
37.   Hebrews 4:12
38.   Hebrews 10:17
39.   Hebrews 12:5-7
40.   James 1:4, 19-20, 4:7-8 & 5:15
41.   1 Peter 2:17, 3:7 & 5:7
42.   1 John 2:14, 4:4 & 4:18
43.   3 John 2
44.   Revelation 12:11

www.ingramcontent.com/pod-product-compliance
Lightning Source LLC
Chambersburg PA
CBHW060523030426
42337CB00015B/1984